KETO
ONE-POT

The One Pot
Ketogenic Diet
Cookbook

THE ONE POT KETOGENIC DIET COOKBOOK

60+ easy to follow ketogenic meals in a single pan

ISBN 978-1-913005-27-6

DISCLAIMER

CONTENTS

KETO ONE-POT VEGETABLE DISHES   49

KETO ONE-POT SEAFOOD DISHES   67

BONUS SECTION: KETO SMOOTHIES & DRINKS   85

CONVERSION CHART   94

INTRODUCTION

The combination of high protein, healthy fats and low carb vegetable ingredients mean meal times don't get much heartier and simpler than one-pot keto meals.

In every country and culture around the world there is a variation of the one-pot meal. In Spain - a paella, France - a boeuf bourguignon, a Moroccan tagine, Italian risotto or a classic Irish stew. Whatever the geography, the concept of cooking delicious meals with minimal preparation, maximum flavour and less cleaning-up is a winning combination. If you are following a Ketogenic diet, the one-pot meal is the perfect way to deliver delicious, calorie controlled, low carb dishes to help you manage your weight.

Whatever the dish used to prepare the meal - be it a casserole, tagine, wok or saucepan – all our recipes require just one-pot to blend flavours together, tenderising ingredients making a flavour packed, wholesome, nutritious and delicious Keto meal that all the family can enjoy.

One-pot Keto meals are particularly good for week-night suppers. Quick to prepare, with no fuss they can be cooked and stored ahead of time ready to warm through for a hearty, perfect meal. The combination of high protein, healthy fats and low carb vegetable ingredients mean meal times don't get much heartier and simpler than one-pot keto dishes.

Based around the principles of the Keto Diet our one-pot recipes have been uniquely designed to help you manage your weight loss and maintain your goal weight, keeping you inspired and feeling energised each step of the way.

What is the Keto Diet?

Unlike many new modern day diets, the Ketogenic, often shortened to 'Keto' Diet has been in existence for almost 100 years. The diet was originally designed for medical purposes by Dr Russell Wilder in 1924 as an effective method of treating epilepsy. The science upon which the diet was based centres around the process whereby the body enters the state of ketosis as a direct result of the consumption of certain foods in a controlled manner. When higher levels of fats are consumed, together with a reduction in carbohydrates, the liver plays its role in converting these natural fats into fatty acids and ketones. An increased quantity of ketones in the blood system enables ketosis. In this state the body uses fat, not carbohydrates as its primary energy source.

When in ketosis, there are a large number of benefits to the body that can help relieve and ease the symptoms of many other diseases and prevent the onset of many others. What is making the Keto Diet evermore popular is the benefit of weight loss that comes with ketosis.

Some benefits of Ketosis

- Appetite is surprised: eating more protein and fats makes you feel fuller for longer.
- Weight loss can be quicker: studies show that cutting carbs is a faster method of shedding excess weight.
- Low carbs can be effective in reducing visceral fat in the abdominal area.
- Increased quantities of healthy fats in your diet can raise levels of HDL (High Density Lipoprotein) which is the 'good' cholesterol.
- Carbs are broken down into sugars which then enter the blood stream. This elevates blood sugar levels and as a result the body produces more insulin to combat this. * By cutting carbs you remove the need for increased insulin which if not correctly managed can lead to Type 2 Diabetes.
- A low carb diet can reduce blood pressure leading to a reduced risk of diseases such as stroke, kidney failure and heart disease.

What foods are 'Keto'?

The Keto Diet is high-fat and low-carb, with a reasonable volume of protein. When the Keto Diet refers to fat, it is simply referring to natural fats, not processed or fast-food fats. There are a number of variations to the Keto Diet if using to treat a specific medical condition (for example epilepsy or Parkinson's), however the majority, if not all, rule out sweets, cakes and treats.

The Keto Diet is largely based around meats, mainly red meats and pork, fatty fish, such as tuna and salmon, chicken and turkey, along with a good balance of eggs and dairy, such as butter, cream and unprocessed cheese. This makes the Keto Diet widely accessible, although it is encouraged that, where possible, meats and other animal products are sourced sustainably to ensure the best quality, such as grass-fed, corn-fed and free range.

Healthy oils, nuts, seeds, and healthy herbs, spices and seasonings are equally as important and can be easily added to any meal. In addition, make sure you fill up your plate with low-carb vegetables such as peppers, tomatoes, onions and largely green vegetables. Whilst fruits tend to be eliminated, the avocado is particularly favoured and beneficial in the Keto Diet.

You will find that some of the recipies in this book do include ingredients which may not be strictly keto. This includes sweet potatoes, soy beans, a little fruit and a dash ot two of wine for cooking. However we would term these type of ingredients as ok to include occasionally but are best avoided during the intial introduction process of the diet.

Why eat Keto?

The Keto Diet not only helps enhance and increase the body's metabolic rate to stimulate weight loss, but it also provides several other health benefits and can be used to relieve and treat the symptoms of some illnesses and conditions when planned and managed properly.

When using the Keto Diet for the purpose of weight loss, unlike so many highly restrictive diets, the Keto Diet provides a significant range of foods that you can eat as part of your programme. This enables you to adopt the

Keto Diet as a lifestyle change because it is sustainable. Many other diets cannot be followed long-term as they eliminate too many food groups, or would risk causing serious damage to the body, particularly 'fasting' diets.

The Keto Diet is a healthy, controlled and balanced way to help you control and maintain your goal weight and this collection of Keto recipes is specifically designed to help manage weight loss.

How to eat Keto

Eating the 'Keto way' and adhering to a Keto Diet is relatively easy. There are different levels of Keto, as such, depending on how strictly you wish to enforce a weight loss approach. Ratios are often referred to in the Keto Diet (for example 60-75% of calories form healthy fats, 15-30% of calories from protein and 5-10% from carbs) to ensure that your food group portions are appropriately proportioned; for example, whilst bacon and red meats can be eaten, a plate of just steak or a stack of bacon rashers is not going to provide improvements alone. Ensuring that your carbohydrate intake is kept as low as possible in conjunction with increased healthy fats and protein can aid quicker and greater weight loss. Moreover, the flexibility that the Keto Diet offers means that once you are happy with a sustained weight, you can become more liberal with your intake and ratios.

How to lose weight with the Keto Diet

Essentially, the fewer carbohydrates you include with your diet, snacks and meals, the greater weight loss you will see!

The Keto Diet looks to exclude sugary foods, such as cake, chocolate and fruit, as well as alcohol. Whilst at first your body will miss and crave these foods, once the sugar is out of your system and you are past the 'withdrawal' stage, your body will crave foods less. Sugary foods do not keep you full for long and are designed to make your body crave more. By eating healthier alternatives including healthy fats within the Keto Diet, you are likely to feel much fuller for longer, experiencing fewer, if any, cravings and also a generally reduced hunger and appetite. Many Keto Diet followers comment on their reduced appetite noting how they easily go longer between meals and rarely snack at all.

When following the Keto Diet, your body uses fat as its energy supply. With lowered sugar levels come lowered insulin levels, which enables and increases the fat burning process even more so, which is how we see weight loss and weight management as such a substantial side effect of a properly planned and managed Keto Diet programme.

When cooking our Keto one-pot meals you should follow these basic principles to achieve the best results:

Saucepans & Casseroles

Good quality dishes do achieve better results that can prevent your dishes from burning and sticking. Use heavy based saucepans and flameproof casserole dishes. Lids are often required for recipes so check before you start.

Meat

Browning meat is very important. You may be tempted to skip this part but the end results will be inferior if you do. Browning meat gives your dish both flavour and colour and by sealing in hot oil it retains its juices. Don't add too much meat to a saucepan when browning – it's better to brown in batches as a build up of steam in a crowded pan will inhibit the browning process.

Part of the joy of one-pot meals that require slower cooking is that tougher cuts of meat can be transformed into delicious and tender bites. The good news for the cook is that cheaper cuts of meat can therefore be used in many recipes.

Trim all meats of any excess fats. While certain cuts of meat such as chicken thighs may be suited to a one-pot recipe, these tend to be much higher in fat and calories so our recipes opt for the leaner cuts of meat wherever possible.

KETO ONE-POT MEAT DISHES

PORK & GREENS

375 calories per serving

Ingredients

- 2 onions, chopped
- 12 slices lean, back bacon, chopped
- 800g/1¾lb green beans/broccoli & shredded Spring Greens
- 2 tbsp tomato puree/paste

- 1 tbsp Dijon mustard
- 1 tbsp red wine vinegar
- 250ml/1 cup chicken stock
- 2 tsp olive oil
- Salt & pepper to taste

Method

1 Preheat the oven to 180c/350f/Gas4

2 Using a flameproof casserole dish gently sauté the onions and chopped bacon in the olive oil for a few minutes until softened.

3 Add all the ingredients to the casserole dish, combine well and bring to a simmer.

4 Cover, transfer to the preheated oven and cook for 1-1 ½ hours or until the stew is bubbling hot and cooked through.

5 Check the stew during cooking. If it needs more liquid add a little stock. If you find there is too much, remove the lid and cook for a little longer to reduce the liquid.

6 Check the seasoning and serve.

CHEFS NOTE
Try to buy charcuterie bacon for this recipe as it has less sugar and processed ingredients.

VEAL & SHALLOT STEW

495 calories per serving

Ingredients

- 2 garlic cloves, crushed
- 500g/2lb 2oz veal, cubed
- 1 tsp smoked paprika
- 2 tbsp tomato puree/paste
- 500g/2lb 2oz shallots
- 120ml/½ cup chicken stock
- 1 tbsp olive oil
- Salt & pepper to taste

Method

1 Using a flameproof casserole dish gently sauté the shallots & garlic in the olive oil until the onions are softened and golden.

2 Remove the shallots from the pan. Increase the heat and quickly fry the cubed veal to seal the meat for just a minute or two.

3 Add all the ingredients into the casserole dish and combine well. Bring to a hard simmer, cover, reduce the heat and leave to gently cook for 20-25 minutes or until the stew is piping hot and everything is cooked though.

4 Check the stew during cooking. If it needs more liquid add a little stock. If you find there is too much, remove the lid and cook for a little longer to reduce the liquid.

5 Ensure the veal is meltingly tender. Check the seasoning and serve.

CHEFS NOTE
Use organic veal which has been reared to the highest animal welfare standards.

SPICED LAMB & ALE STEW

410 calories per serving

Ingredients

- 1 red onion, chopped
- 1 white onion, chopped
- 4 garlic cloves, crushed
- 1 red chilli, deseeded & finely chopped
- 500g/1lb 2oz lean lamb fillet, cubed
- 1 tsp each ground cumin & coriander/ cilantro
- 250ml/1 cup ale
- 1 tbsp balsamic vinegar
- 200g/7oz tinned chopped tomatoes
- 350g/12oz mushrooms, halved
- 2 tsp olive oil
- Salt & pepper to taste

Method

1 Using a flameproof casserole dish gently sauté the onions, garlic & chilli in the olive oil for a few minutes until softened.

2 Remove to a plate, add a little more oil to the casserole dish, increase the heat and quickly brown the lamb for a few minutes.

3 Add all the ingredients, back into the casserole dish and combine well. Bring to a hard simmer, cover, reduce the heat and leave to gently cook for 1 hour or until the stew is piping hot and the lamb is cooked though.

4 Check the stew during cooking. If it needs more liquid add a little stock. If you find there is too much, remove the lid and cook for a little longer to reduce the liquid. Season and serve.

CHEFS NOTE

Although alcohol should be avoided, a little ale in cooking is occasionaly acceptable.

OKRA CHILLI

480
calories per serving

Ingredients

- 1 red onion, chopped
- 1 white onion, chopped
- 2 garlic cloves, crushed
- 2 red pepper, deseeded & sliced
- 1 tsp ground cumin
- 2 tbsp tomato puree/paste
- 400g/14oz tinned chopped tomatoes

- 3 okra, cubed
- 600g/1lb 5oz lean beef mince/ground beef
- 2 sun dried tomatoes, finely chopped
- 120ml/½ cup beef stock
- 2 tsp olive oil
- Salt & pepper to taste

Method

1 Preheat the oven to 180c/350f/Gas4

2 Using a flameproof casserole dish gently sauté the onions, garlic, peppers & sliced okra in the olive oil for a few minutes until softened.

3 Remove to a plate, add a little more oil to the casserole dish, increase the heat and quickly brown the mince for a few minutes.

4 Add all the ingredients back into the casserole dish and combine well. Bring to a hard simmer, cover and place in the preheated oven for 1–1½ hours or until the chilli is piping hot and the mince is cooked though.

5 Check the chilli during cooking. If it needs more liquid add a little stock. If you find there is too much, remove the lid and cook for a little longer to reduce the liquid. Season and serve.

CHEFS NOTE

Okra is thought to help benefit digestive health and vision.

15

SIMPLE BEEF STEW

470
calories per serving

Ingredients

- 500g/1lb 2oz lean chuck steak, cubed
- 1 onion, chopped
- 1 leek, chopped
- 1 celery stalk, chopped
- 2 garlic cloves, crushed
- 125g/4oz mushrooms, sliced
- 2 tbsp almond flour
- 400g/14oz tinned chopped tomatoes
- 2 tbsp Worcestershire sauce
- 500ml/2 cups beef stock
- 1 tbsp Dijon mustard
- 2 tsp olive oil
- Salt & pepper to taste

Method

1 Preheat the oven to 160c/325f/Gas3

2 Using a flameproof casserole dish quickly brown the beef in the olive oil for a few minutes.

3 Remove the beef, add a little more oil and gently sauté the onions, leek, celery, mushrooms & garlic for a few minutes until softened.

4 Stir through the flour until well combined. Add the Worcestershire sauce, stock & mustard and cook for two minutes stirring throughout.

5 Bring to the boil, cover and place in the preheated oven to cook for approximately 2 hours or until the beef is really tender.

6 Check the stew during cooking. If it needs more liquid add a little more stock. If you find there is too much, remove the lid and cook for a little longer to reduce the liquid. Season and serve.

CHEFS NOTE
This stew is lovely served with simple braised cabbage.

NORTHERN STEW

460 calories per serving

Ingredients

- 500g/1lb 2oz lean lamb fillet, cubed
- 2 onions, chopped
- 1 cabbage, chopped
- 1 tbsp almond flour
- 500ml/2 cups beef stock
- 150g/5oz sugar snap peas

- 2 tsp marmite
- 2 tsp mixed dried herbs
- 500g/1lb 2oz sweet potatoes, peeled & cubed
- 2 tsp olive oil
- Salt & pepper to taste

Method

1 Preheat the oven to 160c/325f/Gas3

2 Using a flameproof casserole dish quickly brown the lamb in the olive oil for a few minutes.

3 Remove the lamb, add a little more oil and gently sauté the onions & sweet potatoes for a few minutes until softened.

4 Stir through the flour until well combined. Add the stock and cook for two minutes stirring throughout.

5 Bring to the boil and remove from the heat and . Place in the preheated oven to cook for approximately 2 hours or until the lamb & sweet potatoes are cooked through and tender.

6 Remove the lid for the last half hour of cooking, season and serve.

CHEFS NOTE
Sweet potatoes are fine to use sparingly as an occasional keto ingredient.

BEEF & PUMPKIN ONE-POT

495 calories per serving

Ingredients

- 500g/1lb 2oz lean chuck steak, cubed
- 2 onions, chopped
- 1 celery stalk, chopped
- 1 garlic clove, crushed
- 175g/6oz mushrooms, sliced
- 500ml/2 cups beef stock
- 300g/11oz pumpkin, peeled & diced
- 2 tsp olive oil
- 1 container garden cress
- Salt & pepper to taste

Method

1 Preheat the oven to 160c/325f/Gas3

2 Using a flameproof casserole dish quickly brown the beef in the oil for a few minutes.

3 Remove the beef, add a little more oil and gently sauté the onions, celery, garlic, pumpkin & mushrooms for a few minutes until softened.

4 Add the beef back to the casserole along with the stock.

5 Bring to the boil, cover and place in the preheated oven to cook for approximately 2-2 ½ hours or until the beef is super tender and cooked through.

6 Check the stew during cooking. If it needs more liquid add a little stock. If you find there is too much, remove the lid and cook for a little longer to reduce the liquid.

7 Season and serve with the fresh cress sprinkled over the top of the stew.

CHEFS NOTE
You could also add some almond slivers and grated lemon zest to serve.

18

RABBIT STEW

340 calories per serving

Ingredients

- 500g/1lb 2oz diced fresh rabbit
- 2 onions, chopped
- 1 celery stalk, chopped
- 1 garlic clove, crushed
- 75g/3oz spinach, chopped
- 1 tbsp Worcestershire sauce

- 400g/14oz vine ripened tomatoes, roughly chopped
- 500ml/2 cups beef stock
- 2 tsp olive oil
- Salt & pepper to taste

Method

1 Preheat the oven to 160c/325f/Gas3. Using a flameproof casserole dish quickly brown the rabbit in the olive oil for a few minutes.

2 Remove the rabbit, add a little more oil and gently sauté the onions, celery & garlic for a few minutes until softened.

3 Add the rabbit back to the casserole along with the Worcestershire sauce, tomatoes & stock.

4 Bring to the boil, cover and place in the preheated oven to cook for approximately 2-2 ½ hours or until the meat is super tender and cooked through.

5 Check the stew during cooking. If it needs more liquid add a little stock. If there's too much, remove the lid and cook for longer to reduce the liquid.

6 A minute or two before serving add the spinach and stir through until wilted.

7 Season and serve.

CHEFS NOTE
Rabbit is a great meat for stewing and is widely availible in most large stores.

19

SAGE PORK

390 calories per serving

Ingredients

- 600g/1lb 5oz pork tenderloin, cubed
- 2 onions, chopped
- 1 celery stalk, chopped
- 1 garlic clove, crushed
- 2 tsp anchovy paste

- 2 apples, peeled, cored and diced
- 2 tbsp fresh sage, chopped
- 500ml/2 cups chicken stock
- 2 tsp olive oil
- Salt & pepper to taste

Method

1 Preheat the oven to 160c/325f/Gas3

2 Using a flameproof casserole dish quickly brown the pork in the olive oil for a few minutes. Remove the pork, add a little more oil and gently sauté the onions, celery & garlic for a few minutes until softened.

3 Add the pork back to the dish along with all the other ingredients. Bring to the boil, cover and place in the preheated oven for approximately 2 - 2 ½ hours or until the pork is tender and the apples are pulpy.

4 Check the stew during cooking. If it needs more liquid add a little stock. If you find there is too much, remove the lid and cook for a little longer to reduce the liquid. Season and serve.

CHEFS NOTE
Cooking apples are best in this recipe.

SIMPLE SPANISH STEW

480
calories per
serving

Ingredients

- 1 onion, chopped
- 3 garlic cloves, crushed
- 150g/5oz chorizo, finely chopped
- 1 red pepper, deseeded & sliced
- 200g/7oz cherry tomatoes, halved
- 200g/7oz skinless chicken breasts, sliced
- ½ tsp cayenne pepper

- 500ml/2 cups chicken stock
- 1 tsp turmeric
- 200g/7oz pumpkin, finely chopped
- 150g/5oz grean beans
- 200g/7oz raw shelled prawns, chopped
- 1 tsp olive oil
- Salt & pepper to taste

Method

1 Using a heavy bottomed frying pan gently sauté the onions, garlic, chorizo, peppers, chopped pumpkin & cherry tomatoes in the olive oil for a few minutes until softened.

2 Add the chicken and cook for 2 minutes longer.

3 Add the cayenne pepper, stock & turmeric.. Bring to the boil, cover and cook for 30 minutes.

4 Add the green beans and prawns, cover and leave to simmer for a further 8-10 minutes or until the stock has been absorbed and the prawns are cooked through.

5 Check during cooking. If it needs more liquid add additional stock. Season and serve.

CHEFS NOTE

Almost any mix of meats and seafood will work well in this versatile Spanish stew.

SHREDDED LAMB

495 calories per serving

Ingredients

- 600g/1lb 5oz lean lamb shoulder, trimmed
- 1 tsp dried rosemary
- Pinch salt
- 3 tbsp lemon juice
- 1 tbsp each olive oil and balsamic vinegar
- 2 garlic cloves, crushed
- 1 onion, sliced
- 400g/14oz tinned chopped tomatoes
- 300g/11oz butternut squash, finel chopped
- 120ml/½ cup chicken stock
- Salt & pepper to taste

Method

1 Preheat the oven to 160c/325f/Gas3

2 Mix together the rosemary, salt, lemon juice, olive oil, balsamic vinegar & garlic. Rub this all over the lamb and season well.

3 Sit the lamb in a flameproof casserole dish and add the onions, tomatoes, squash & stock around the sides of the lamb. Cover and place in a preheated oven for approx 2-3 hours or until the lamb is very tender.

4 Check the stew during cooking. If it needs more liquid add a little stock.

5 Turn the lamb half way through cooking to ensure it doesn't dry out. When the cooking time is over allow the lamb to cool for a little while and then use your hands, or two forks, to shred into thin strips.

6 Spoon out the tomatoes and veg into shallow bowls and sit the shredded lamb on top. Check the seasoning and serve.

CHEFS NOTE
Lamb on the bone is good for this recipe. The weight in the ingredients is for meat only. A bone-in joint will be heavier.

BEEF & MUSTARD STEW

439
calories per serving

Ingredients

- 500g/1lb 2oz lean chuck steak, cubed
- 2 garlic cloves, crushed
- 2 onions, chopped
- 125g/4oz mushrooms, sliced
- 1 tbsp plain/almond flour
- 500ml/2 cups beef stock
- 1 tbsp Dijon mustard
- 1 tsp English mustard
- 1 tsp dried thyme
- 2 tsp brown sugar
- 300g/11oz sweet potatoes, peeled & diced
- 2 tsp olive oil
- Salt & pepper to taste

Method

1 Preheat the oven to 160c/325f/Gas3

2 Using a flameproof casserole dish quickly brown the beef in the olive oil for a few minutes. Remove the beef, add a little more oil and gently sauté the onions, garlic & mushrooms for a few minutes until softened (add a splash of water if it's a little dry). Stir through the flour and cook for a minute or two longer.

3 Add the stock, both mustards, sugar, thyme, sweet potatoes and browned beef. Bring to the boil, cover and place in the preheated oven to cook for approximately 1½-2 hours, or until the beef is super tender and cooked through.

4 Check the stew during cooking. If it needs more liquid add a little stock. If you find there is too much, remove the lid and cook for a little longer to reduce the liquid. Season and serve.

CHEFS NOTE
Sweet potatoes should only be used occasionally on a keto diet.

GREEK BEEF STEW

490 calories per serving

Ingredients

- 500g/1lb 2oz lean chuck steak, cubed
- 2 red onions, quartered
- 2 artichokes, chopped
- 2 celery stalks, roughly sliced
- 2 tbsp freshly chopped oregano
- 400g/14oz tinned chopped tomatoes
- 2 tbsp tomato puree/paste

- ½ tsp ground cinnamon
- 2 tbsp raisins, chopped
- 2 tsp olive oil
- Zest of one lemon
- 75g/3oz feta cheese, crumbled
- Salt & pepper to taste

Method

1 Preheat the oven to 160c/325f/Gas3

2 Using a flameproof casserole dish quickly brown the beef in the olive oil for a few minutes. Remove the beef, add a little more oil and gently sauté the onions, artichokes & chopped celery for a few minutes until softened (add a splash of water.

3 Add the browned beef, oregano, tomatoes, tomato puree, cinnamon & raisins.

4 Bring to the boil, cover and place in the preheated oven to cook for approximately 1½-2 hours, or until the beef is super tender and cooked through.

5 Check the stew during cooking. If it needs more liquid add a little stock. If you find there is too much, remove the lid and cook for a little longer to reduce the liquid. Season and serve with lemon zest and feta cheese sprinkled over the top of the stew.

CHEFS NOTE
You could try orange zest as a garnish too if you wish.

RED WINE BEEF

460 calories per serving

Ingredients

- 500g/1lb 2oz lean chuck steak, cubed
- 2 onions, chopped
- 250g/9oz mushrooms, sliced
- 500ml/2 cups red wine
- 8 garlic cloves, peeled and left whole
- 1 tsp dried rosemary
- 1 tsp ground black pepper
- 2 tsp olive oil spray
- Salt & pepper to taste

Method

1 Preheat the oven to 150c/300f/Gas2

2 Using a flameproof casserole dish quickly brown the beef in the olive oil for a few minutes. Remove the beef, add a little more oil and gently sauté the onions & mushrooms for a few minutes until softened..

3 Add the browned beef, red wine, garlic cloves, rosemary & black pepper. Bring to the boil, cover and place in the preheated oven to cook for approximately 2-2½ hours, or until the beef is super tender and cooked through.

4 Check the stew during cooking. If it needs more liquid add a little stock. If you find there is too much, remove the lid and cook for a little longer to reduce the liquid. Season and serve.

CHEFS NOTE
Alcohol is not recommended on a keto diet, however using red wine occasionally in cooking is acceptable..

BEEF & PORTABELLA STROGANOFF

380 calories per serving

Ingredients

- 500g/1lb 2oz lean chuck steak, cubed
- 2 onions, chopped
- 4 portabella mushrooms, thickly sliced
- 180ml/¾ cup beef stock
- 2 tbsp tomato puree/paste
- 2 tsp paprika
- 120ml/½ crème fraiche
- 2 tsp olive oil
- Salt & pepper to taste

Method

1 Preheat the oven to 160c/325f/Gas3

2 Using a flameproof casserole dish quickly brown the beef in the live oil for a few minutes.

3 Remove the beef, add a little more oil and gently sauté the onions & mushrooms for a few minutes until softened.

4 Add the browned beef, stock, puree & paprika. Bring to the boil, cover and place in the preheated oven to cook for approximately 1½-2 hours, or until the beef is super tender and cooked through.

5 Check the stew during cooking. If it needs more liquid add a little stock. If you find there is too much, remove the lid and cook for a little longer to reduce the liquid.

6 Stir through the crème fraiche, season and serve.

CHEFS NOTE
Serve with steamed shredded cabbage and cauliflower if you wish.

CLASSIC SHALLOT BOURGUIGNON

440 calories per serving

Ingredients

- 500g/1lb 2oz lean chuck steak, cubed
- 2 onions, chopped
- 2 slices lean, back bacon, chopped
- 3 garlic cloves, crushed
- 300g/11oz chestnut mushrooms, halved
- 1 tbsp almond flour
- 1 tsp dried thyme
- 370ml/1 ½ cups beef stock

- 50g/2oz butter
- 10 shallots, peeled & halved
- 2 tsp olive oil
- Handful of freshly chopped flat leaf parsley
- Salt & pepper to taste

Method

1 Preheat the oven to 160c/325f/Gas3

2 Using a flameproof casserole dish quickly brown the beef in the olive oil for a few minutes. Remove the beef, add a little more oil and gently sauté the onions, bacon, garlic & mushrooms for a few minutes until softened.

3 Place the beef in a plastic bag with the flour and shake until the beef is lightly covered in all the flour.

4 Add the floured beef, thyme & stock. Bring to the boil, cover and place in the preheated oven to cook for approximately 1½-2 hours, or until the beef is super tender and cooked through.

5 Check the stew during cooking. If it needs more liquid add a little stock. If you find there is too much, remove the lid and cook for a little longer to reduce the liquid.

6 As the stew nears the end of it's cooking time gently sauté the shallots in a frying pan with the butter for at least 10 minutes on a very gentle heat to caramelise.

7 When the stew is ready stir through the shallots, check the seasoning and serve with chopped parsley.

SMOKED HAM & CREAM CHEESE 'RISOTTO'

350 calories per serving

Ingredients

- 1 tbsp olive oil
- 1 onion, chopped
- 1 leek, sliced
- 1 garlic clove, crushed
- 1 large cauliflower

- 125g/4oz smoked ham, chopped
- 200g/7oz peas
- 120g/½ cup vegetable stock
- 3 tbsp cream cheese
- Salt & pepper to taste

Method

1 Preheat the oven to 180c/350f/Gas4

2 Using a flameproof casserole dish gently sauté the onion, leek & garlic in the olive oil for about 5 minutes until softened.

3 Add the ham, peas & stock and bring to the boil.

4 Meanwhile break up the cauliflower and 'whizz' in a food processor to make cauliflower 'rice'

5 Add the rice to the casserole dish. Cover and place in the preheated oven for 25-30 minutes or until the stock has been absorbed.

6 Check during cooking. If it needs more liquid add a little stock. If you find there is too much, remove the lid and cook for a little longer to reduce the stock.

7 Remove from the oven, stir through the cream cheese, season & serve.

CHEFS NOTE
Cauliflower 'rice' makes a good keto alternative to risotto rice.

SAUSAGE GOULASH

430 calories per serving

Ingredients

- 8 lean pork sausages
- 2 onions, chopped
- 2 garlic cloves, crushed
- 1 red pepper, deseeded & sliced
- 200g/7oz chestnut mushrooms, halved
- 1 tsp paprika
- ½ tsp cayenne pepper or chilli powder
- 1 tbsp almond flour

- 400g/14oz tinned chopped tomatoes
- 250ml/1 cup beef stock
- 4 tbsp Greek yogurt
- 1 tsp olive oil
- Handful of freshly chopped flat leaf parsley
- Salt & pepper to taste

Method

1 Preheat the oven to 160c/325f/Gas3

2 Using a flameproof casserole dish quickly brown the sausages in the olive oil for a few minutes. Remove the sausages and slice into 1cm/½ inch thick rounds.

3 Add a little more oil to the casserole and gently sauté the onions, garlic, peppers & mushrooms for a few minutes until softened. Stir through the flour, paprika & cayenne pepper and cook for a minute or two longer. Add the sliced sausages, tomatoes & stock.

4 Quickly bring to the boil, cover and place in the preheated oven to cook for approximately 1-1½ hours, or until the stew is thick and piping hot.

5 Check the stew during cooking. If it needs more liquid add a little stock. If you find there is too much, remove the lid and cook for a little longer to reduce the liquid.

6 Season and serve with a tablespoon of Greek yogurt on top sprinkled with chopped parsley.

CHEFS NOTE
Use sausages which do not contain fillers such as gluten, rusk or soya.

VENISON COCONUT STEW

500 calories per serving

Ingredients

- 600g/1lb 5oz venison, cubed
- 1 onion, sliced
- 2 peppers, deseeded & sliced
- 1 tbsp freshly grated ginger
- 1 red chilli, deseeded & finely sliced
- 3 tbsp Thai fish sauce

- 400g/14oz tinned chopped tomatoes
- 120ml/½ cup beef stock
- 250ml/1 cup coconut milk
- Lime wedges to serve
- 2 tsp olive oil
- Salt & pepper to taste

Method

1 Using a flameproof casserole dish quickly brown the venison in the olive oil for a couple of minutes.

2 Remove the meat, add a little more oil and gently sauté the onions, peppers, ginger & chilli for a few minutes until softened

3 Add the fish sauce, sugar, chopped tomatoes & stock. Bring to the boil, cover and leave to gently simmer for an hour. Stir through the coconut milk and continue to gently simmer for a few minutes until the beef is tender and the stew is piping hot.

4 Check the stew during cooking. If it needs more liquid add a little stock. If you find there is too much, remove the lid and cook for a little longer to reduce the liquid. Season and serve with lime wedges

CHEFS NOTE
Try serving with some chopped peanuts and fresh coriander.

LAMB POT

460
calories per
serving

Ingredients

- 2 aubergine/egg plant, sliced
- 500g/1lb 2oz lean lamb shoulder, cubed
- 2 onions, sliced
- 3 garlic cloves, crushed
- 400g/14oz tinned chopped tomatoes
- 1 tbsp curry powder
- 120ml/½ cup chicken stock
- 125g/4oz sugar snap peas
- Small bunch freshly chopped coriander/cilantro
- 2 tsp olive oil
- Salt & pepper to taste

Method

1 Using a flameproof casserole dish quickly brown the lamb in the olive oil for a couple of minutes.

2 Remove the lamb, add a little more oil and gently sauté the onions, aubergine & garlic for a few minutes until softened.

3 Add the tomatoes, curry powder & stock. Bring to the boil, cover and leave to gently simmer for at least an hour or until the lamb is tender and the lentils are cooked through.

4 Add the peas 5-10 minutes before the end of cooking time.

5 Check the stew during cooking. If it needs more liquid add a little stock. If you find there is too much, remove the lid and cook for a little longer to reduce the liquid. Season and serve with freshly chopped coriander.

CHEFS NOTE

Adjust the amount of curry powder to suit your own taste.

MOROCCAN LAMB & ONIONS

440 calories per serving

Ingredients

- 500g/1lb 2oz lean lamb shoulder, cubed
- 3 onions, sliced
- 3 garlic cloves, crushed
- 400g/14oz tomatoes, roughly chopped
- 2 tbsp tomato puree/paste
- 1 tbsp honey
- 1 tsp each ground coriander/cilantro & turmeric
- ½ tsp each ground cinnamon & allspice
- 50g/2oz dried apricots, chopped
- 1 large sweet potato, peeled & diced
- 2 tbsp raisins, chopped
- 120ml/½ cup chicken stock
- 2 tsp olive oil
- Salt & pepper to taste

Method

1 Using a flameproof casserole dish quickly brown the lamb in the olive oil for a couple of minutes.

2 Remove the lamb, add a little more oil and gently sauté the onions & garlic for about 10 minutes until very soft .

3 Add the tomatoes, puree, honey, dried spices, apricots, sweet potato, raisins & stock. Bring to the boil, cover and leave to gently simmer for 1-1 ½ hours or until the lamb is very tender.

4 Check the stew during cooking. If it needs more liquid add a little stock. If you find there is too much, remove the lid and cook for a little longer to reduce the liquid. Season and serve.

CHEFS NOTE

Honey & sweet potato are acceptable 'occasional' keto cooking ingredients.

BEEF & KALE STEW

460 calories per serving

Ingredients

- 1 tbsp almond flour
- 500g/1lb 2oz lean chuck steak, cubed
- 2 onions, sliced
- 2 garlic cloves, crushed
- 150g/5oz kale chopped
- 500ml/2 cups beef stock
- 1 butternut squash, peeled, deseeded & cubed
- 2 tsp olive oil
- Salt & pepper to taste

Method

1 Dust the beef with flour. Using a flameproof casserole dish quickly brown the floured beef in the olive oil for a couple of minutes.

2 Remove the beef, add a little more oil and gently sauté the onions & garlic for a few minutes until softened.

3 Add the stock, kale & squash. Bring to the boil, cover and leave to gently simmer for 1½-2 hours or until the beef is very tender and the stew is piping hot.

4 Check the stew during cooking. If it needs more liquid add a little stock. If you find there is too much, remove the lid and cook for a little longer to reduce the liquid. Season and serve.

CHEFS NOTE
Place the flour and steak in a plastic bag and shake to evenly cover the beef.

SPICED PORK & OLIVE STEW

380 calories per serving

Ingredients

- 500g/1lb 2oz pork tenderloin, cubed
- 1 onion, chopped
- 1 red chilli, deseeded & finely chopped
- 2 garlic cloves, crushed
- 3 slices lean, back bacon, chopped
- 75g/3oz olives, sliced
- 400g/14oz vine ripened tomatoes, chopped
- 50g/2oz spinach, chopped
- 60ml/¼ cup chicken stock
- 2 tsp olive oil
- Salt & pepper to taste

Method

1 Using a flameproof casserole dish quickly brown the pork in the olive oil for a couple of minutes. Remove the pork, add a little more oil and gently sauté the onions, chilli, garlic & chopped bacon for a few minutes until softened.

2 Add all the ingredients to the casserole dish, combine well and bring to a simmer. Cover and cook for 45–60 mins or until the stew is bubbling hot and cooked through.

3 Check often during cooking. If it needs more liquid add a little stock. If you find there is too much, remove the lid and cook for a little longer to reduce the liquid. Season and serve.

CHEFS NOTE
Chopped almonds and a dollop of full fat yoghurt make a good serving garnish.

NO 'PILAF' ONE-POT

380 calories per serving

Ingredients

- 1 onion, chopped
- 2 garlic cloves, crushed
- 1 tsp each ground cumin, turmeric & chilli powder
- 500g/1lb 2oz lean minced/ground beef

- 150g/5oz green beans, chopped
- 250ml/1 cup beef stock
- 2 tsp olive oil
- Salt & pepper to taste

Method

1 Using a flameproof casserole dish gently sauté the onions & garlic in a little low cal spray for a few minutes until the onions are softened.

2 Add the dried spices & beef and cook for a few minutes. Add the green beans & stock. Cover and gently simmer for 15-20 minutes or until the stock is absorbed.

3 Check the 'pilaf' during cooking. If it needs more liquid add a little stock. If you find there is too much, remove the lid and cook for a little longer to reduce the liquid. Season and serve.

CHEFS NOTE
Chopped coriander/cilantro makes a good garnish for this dish.

KETO
ONE-POT
POULTRY
DISHES

CHICKEN & CHORIZO STEW

490 calories per serving

Ingredients

- 1 onion, chopped
- 2 garlic cloves, crushed
- 200g/7oz chorizo, sliced & chopped
- 1 red pepper, deseeded & sliced
- 1 red chilli, deseeded & finely chopped
- 4 skinless chicken breasts, each weighing 150g/5oz
- 400g/14oz tinned chopped tomatoes

- 120ml/½ cups chicken stock
- 2 tbsp tomato puree/paste
- 2 bay leaves
- Lemon wedges to serve
- 1 tsp olive oil
- Salt & pepper to taste

Method

1 Using a flameproof casserole dish gently sauté the onions, garlic, chorizo, pepper & chopped chillies in the olive oil for a few minutes until softened.

2 Remove to a plate, add a little more oil to the casserole dish, increase the heat and quickly brown the chicken breasts for a few minutes.

3 Add all the ingredients back into the casserole dish and combine well. Bring to a hard simmer, cover, reduce the heat and leave to gently cook for 20-25 minutes or the chicken is cooked through.

4 Check the stew during cooking. If it needs more liquid add a little stock. If you find there is too much, remove the lid and cook for a little longer to reduce the liquid.

5 Remove the bay leaves, check the seasoning and serve with lemon wedges.

CHEFS NOTE
Try shredding the chicken breasts after cooking and stir back through the stew.

COCONUT MILK & CHICKEN LIGHT STEW

295 calories per serving

Ingredients

- 1 onion, chopped
- 2 garlic cloves, crushed
- 1 red chilli, deseeded & finely chopped
- 400g/14oz skinless chicken breast, cubed
- 250g/9oz sugar snap peas
- 200g/7oz cherry tomatoes, halved
- 2 tbsp tomato puree/paste

- 120ml/½ cup low fat coconut milk
- Small bunch fresh coriander/cilantro, roughly chopped
- 1 tsp olive oil
- 75g/3oz spinach, chopped
- Salt & pepper to taste

Method

1 Using a flameproof casserole dish gently sauté the onions, garlic & chopped chillies in the olive oil for a few minutes until softened.

2 Remove to a plate, add a little more oil to the casserole dish, increase the heat and quickly brown the chicken for a few minutes.

3 Add all the sautéed vegetables, peas, cherry tomatoes & puree back into the casserole dish and combine well. Gently cook for 5 minutes. Add the coconut milk & chopped coriander, cover and leave to gently cook for 20-25 minutes or until the stew is piping hot and the chicken is cooked through.

4 Check the stew during cooking. If it needs more liquid add a little stock. If you find there is too much, remove the lid and cook for a little longer to reduce the liquid.

5 Stir through the spinach to wilt. Check the seasoning and serve with lime wedges.

CHEFS NOTE
Reserve a little of the chopped coriander to use as a garnish.

CHICKEN & ROSEMARY

298
calories per
serving

Ingredients

- 1 onion, chopped
- 1 leek, chopped
- 1 celery stalk, chopped
- 2 handfuls olives, sliced
- 2 garlic cloves, crushed
- 4 skinless chicken breasts, each weighing 125g/4oz
- 1 tbsp almond flour

- 500g/2 cups chicken stock
- 1 tbsp Dijon mustard
- Small bunch fresh rosemary, roughly chopped
- 200g/7oz green beans
- 2 handfuls shredded cabbage or spring greens
- 2 tsp olove oil
- Salt & pepper to taste

Method

1 Using a flameproof casserole dish quickly brown the chicken breasts in the olive oil for a couple of minutes. Remove the chicken, add a little more oil and gently sauté the onions, leek, celery & garlic for a few minutes until softened

2 Stir through the flour until well combined.

3 Add the stock & mustard and cook for two minutes stirring throughout. Add the rosemary and olives, cover and leave to gently cook for 40-50 minutes or until the stew is piping hot and the chicken is cooked through.

4 Five minutes before the end of cooking add the green beans and cabbage (add earlier if you prefer them tender rather than crunchy).

5 Check the stew during cooking. If it needs more liquid add a little stock. If you find there is too much, remove the lid and cook for a little longer to reduce the liquid.

6 Check the seasoning and serving.

CHEFS NOTE

A tablespoon of Greek yogurt makes a good addition to this stew when serving.

CHICKEN & APPLE JUICE CASSEROLE

340 calories per serving

Ingredients

- 4 skinless chicken breasts, each weighing 150g/5oz
- 2 onions, chopped
- 4 garlic cloves, crushed
- 200g/7oz broccoli
- 200g/7oz mushrooms, sliced
- 250ml/1 cup apple juice
- 120ml/½ cup chicken stock
- Lemon wedges to serve
- 2 tsp olive oil
- Salt & pepper to taste

Method

1 Using a flameproof casserole dish quickly brown the chicken in the olive oil for a few minutes.

2 Remove the chicken to a plate, add a little more oil and gently sauté the onions, garlic, broccoli & mushrooms for a few minutes until softened.

3 Add the chicken and apple juice to the casserole and bring to the boil for 2 minutes. Add the stock, cover and gently simmer for 20-30 minutes or until the chicken is cooked through.

4 Check the stew during cooking. If it needs more liquid add a little stock. If you find there is too much, remove the lid and cook for a little longer to reduce the liquid. Season and serve.

CHEFS NOTE

This stew is great served with mashed sweet potatoes and chopped parsley.

FRESH TOMATO & BASIL ONE-POT CHICKEN

345 calories per serving

Ingredients

- 2 onions, chopped
- 6 garlic cloves, crushed
- 600g/1lb 5oz vine ripened tomatoes, roughly chopped
- 4 skinless chicken breasts, each weighing 150g/5oz
- 120ml/½ cup red grape juice
- 120ml/½ cup chicken stock
- Large bunch fresh basil, chopped
- 1 bay leaf
- 1 tsp olive oil
- Salt & pepper to taste

Method

1 Using a flameproof casserole dish, gently sauté the onions, garlic & tomatoes for a few minutes until softened.

2 Add the chicken, grape juice, basil & bay leaf and bring to the boil for 2 minutes. Add the stock, cover and gently simmer for 30-40 minutes or until the chicken is cooked through and tender.

3 Check the stew during cooking. If it needs more liquid add a little stock. If you find there is too much, remove the lid and cook for a little longer to reduce the liquid. Season and serve.

CHEFS NOTE
Reserve a little of the basil as a garnish.

AROMATIC CHICKEN STEW

370 calories per serving

Ingredients

- 400g/14oz skinless chicken breasts, cubed
- 2 onions, sliced
- 3 garlic cloves, crushed
- 2 peppers, sliced
- 1 tsp each turmeric & cumin

- ½ tsp each ground cinnamon & cardamom
- 250ml/1 cup chicken stock
- 2 tbsp chopped raisins
- 2 tsp olive oil
- Salt & pepper to taste

Method

1 Preheat the oven to 180c/350f/Gas4

2 Using a flameproof casserole dish gently sauté the onions & garlic in the olive oil for a few minutes until softened.

3 Add all the ingredients to the casserole, combine well and bring to the boil. Cover the casserole dish, transfer to the preheated oven and cook for 1-1 ½ hours or until the the chicken is cooked through.

4 Check the stew during cooking. If it needs more liquid add a little stock. If you find there is too much, remove the lid and cook for a little longer to reduce the liquid. Season and serve.

CHEFS NOTE

Try serving this with cauliflower 'rice' and chopped coriander.

SPICED CHICKEN & OLIVES

460 calories per serving

Ingredients

- 500g/1lb 2oz skinless chicken breasts, cubed
- 2 onions, sliced
- 3 garlic cloves, crushed
- 2 green chillies, deseeded & finely chopped
- 1 tsp turmeric
- ½ tsp cayenne pepper
- 200g/7oz pumpkin, cubed
- 50g/2oz black, pitted olives, halved
- 400g/14oz tinned chopped tomatoes
- 120ml/½ cup chicken stock
- 2 tbsp Greek yogurt
- 2 tsp olive oil
- Salt & pepper to taste

Method

1 Using a flameproof casserole dish quickly brown the chicken in the oil for a couple of minutes.

2 Remove the chicken to a plate, add a little more oil and gently sauté the onions, garlic, pumpkin & chilli for a few minutes until softened Add the turmeric, cayenne pepper, olives, tomatoes & stock. Bring to the boil, cover and leave to gently simmer cook for 30 minutes or until the chicken is tender.

3 Check the stew during cooking. If it needs more liquid add a little stock. If you find there is too much, remove the lid and cook for a little longer to reduce the liquid.

4 Stir through the yogurt until gently warmed, season and serve.

CHEFS NOTE
Use pitted Kalamata olives if you can get them.

44

HONEY MUSTARD CHICKEN

320 calories per serving

Ingredients

- 4 chicken breasts, each weighing 5oz/150g
- 2 onions, sliced
- 1 red pepper, deseeded & sliced
- 2 garlic cloves, crushed
- 250g/9oz asparagus
- 1 tbsp honey
- 250ml/1 cup chicken stock
- 1 tsp dried thyme
- 2 tsp olive oil
- Salt & pepper to taste

Method

1 Using a flameproof casserole dish quickly brown the chicken in the oil for a couple of minutes.

2 Remove the chicken, add a little more oil and gently sauté the onions, peppers & garlic for a few minutes until softened.

3 Add the honey, stock and thyme. Bring to the boil, cover and leave to gently simmer for about 40 mins or until the chicken is cooked through.

4 Check during cooking. If it needs more liquid add a little stock. If you find there is too much, remove the lid and cook for a little longer to reduce the liquid.

5 Add the aspargus 10 minutes before seasoning & serving.

CHEFS NOTE
This is great served with a mound of steamed savoy cabbage.

AFRICAN CHICKEN ONE-POT

495 calories per serving

Ingredients

- 500g/1lb 2oz skinless chicken breasts, cubed
- 1 red onion, sliced
- 3 garlic cloves, crushed
- 2 tsp freshly grated ginger
- 2 red chillies, deseeded & finely chopped
- 400g/14oz tinned chopped tomatoes
- 125g/4oz 100% natural peanut butter

- 120ml/½ cup chicken stock
- 300g/11oz sweet potatoes, peeled & cubed
- 100g/3½oz sugar snap peas
- 125g/4oz watercress
- 2 tsp olive oil
- Salt & pepper to taste

Method

1 Using a flameproof casserole dish quickly brown the chicken in the oil for a couple of minutes.

2 Remove the chicken, add a little more oil and gently sauté the onions, garlic, ginger & chillies for a few minutes until softened.

3 Add the tomatoes, peanut butter, stock, sweet potatoes & peas. Bring to the boil, cover and leave to gently simmer cook for 30 minutes or until the chicken is tender.

4 Check the stew during cooking. If it needs more liquid add a little stock. If you find there is too much, remove the lid and cook for a little longer to reduce the liquid. Season and serve with a pile of fresh watercress.

CHEFS NOTE
Sweet potatoes are an acceptable occasional keto ingredient.

TURKEY CASSEROLE

410 calories per serving

Ingredients

- 3 slices lean, back bacon, chopped
- 500g/1lb 2oz turkey breasts, chopped
- 1 onion, sliced
- 1 red pepper, deseeded & sliced
- 1 garlic clove, crushed
- 2 tbsp tomato puree/paste
- 250ml/1 cup chicken stock
- 200g/7oz black soy beans
- 1 tsp dried thyme
- 2 tsp olive oil
- Salt & pepper to taste

Method

1 Using a flameproof casserole dish quickly brown the bacon and turkey in the oil for a couple of minutes.

2 Remove the bacon and turkey to a plate, add a little more oil and gently sauté the onions, peppers & garlic for a few minutes until softened.

3 Add the puree, stock, soy beans and thyme. Bring to the boil, cover and leave to gently simmer for about 40 mins or until the beans are tender and the stock has reduced.

4 Check the casserole during cooking. If it needs more liquid add a little stock. If you find there is too much, remove the lid and cook for a little longer to reduce the liquid. Season and serve.

CHEFS NOTE
Black soy beans are acceptable for keto cooking as they are very low carb.

KETO
ONE-POT
VEGETABLE
DISHES

BLACK BEAN TAGINE

SERVES 4

360 calories per serving

Ingredients

- 1 onion, chopped
- 2 garlic cloves, crushed
- 1 red pepper, deseeded & sliced
- 1 aubergine/egg plant, cubed
- 1 red chilli, deseeded & finely chopped
- 3 large vine ripened tomatoes, chopped
- 1 tsp ground paprika
- 2 tbsp tomato puree/paste

- 250ml/1 cup vegetable stock
- ½ tsp ground coriander/cilantro
- 800g/1¾lb tinned black soy beans, drained
- 4 tbsp Greek yogurt
- 2 tsp olive oil
- Salt & pepper to taste

Method

1 Using a flameproof casserole dish gently sauté the onions, garlic, peppers, aubergine, chillies & tomatoes in the oil for about 10 minutes until softened.

2 Add the paprika, puree, stock & coriander. Cover and gently simmer for 10 minutes.

3 Add the beans and cook for a further 20 minutes or until everything is tender and piping hot.

4 Check the beans during cooking. If they need more liquid add a little stock. If you find there is too much, remove the lid and cook for a little longer to reduce the liquid.

5 Season and serve with a dollop of fat free Greek yogurt on top.

CHEFS NOTE
Black soy beans are a good Keto staple.

50

WHITE KIDNEY BEANS & PAK CHOI

380 calories per serving

Ingredients

- 1 onion, chopped
- 2 garlic cloves, crushed
- 1 red pepper, deseeded & sliced
- 1 green chilli, deseeded & finely chopped
- 1 tbsp curry powder
- 1 tsp each turmeric & cumin
- 400g/14oz tinned, chopped tomatoes
- 250ml/1 cup vegetable stock
- 2 tbsp tomato puree/paste
- 800g/1¾lb tinned white kidney beans, drained
- 2 pak choi, shredded
- 2 tsp olive oil
- Salt & pepper to taste

Method

1 Preheat the oven to 180c/350f/Gas4

2 Using a flameproof casserole dish gently sauté the onions, garlic, peppers & chill in the olive oil for a few minutes until softened.

3 Add the curry powder, turmeric, cumin, chopped tomatoes, stock, puree & kidney beans. Combine well and bring to the boil.

4 Cover the casserole dish, transfer to the preheated oven and cook for 1-1 ½ hours or until the stew is bubbling hot and cooked through.

5 Check the stew during cooking. If it needs more liquid add a little stock. If you find there is too much, remove the lid and cook for a little longer to reduce the liquid.

6 Stir through the shredded pak choi, check the seasoning and serve.

CHEFS NOTE

White kidney beans are a good 'occasional' low carb option.

CREAMY BUTTERNUT SQUASH STEW

400 calories per serving

Ingredients

- 2 butternut squash, peeled & deseeded
- 2 onions, chopped
- 2 garlic cloves, crushed
- 5 radishes, finely chopped
- 1 tsp dried rosemary
- 250g/9oz enoki mushrooms
- 1lt/4 cups vegetable stock
- 60ml/¼ cup single cream
- 2 tsp olive oil
- Salt & pepper to taste

Method

1 Cut the squash into chunks.

2 Using a flameproof casserole dish gently sauté the onions, garlic & rosemary in the oil for about 10 minutes until softened.

3 Add the mushrooms, stock & squash chunks. Cover and gently simmer for 40-50 minutes or until the the squash is cooked through.

4 Check during cooking. If it needs more liquid add a little stock. If you find there is too much, remove the lid and cook for a little longer to reduce the liquid.

5 Remove a ladle of the stew and blitz in a food processor until smooth (this will create a thicker, creamier texture to the stew). Return to the stew, stir through the cream and serve with the chopped radishes on top.

CHEFS NOTE

This is a super creamy stew, which is lovely served with salad.

CINNAMON ARTICHOKES

480
calories per
serving

Ingredients

- 1 onion, chopped
- 2 garlic cloves, crushed
- 4 artichokes, chopped
- 1 tsp dried mixed herbs
- 400g/14oz tinned black soy beans
- 500ml/2 cups vegetable stock
- 1 tsp ground cinnamon
- 1 red onion, sliced
- 200g/7oz cherry tomatoes, halved
- 4 tsp olive oil
- Salt & pepper to taste

Method

1 Using a flameproof casserole dish gently sauté the onions, garlic, artichokes & dried herbs in 1 tsp of the olive oil for a few minutes until softened.

2 Add the soy beans, stock & cinnamon. Cover and gently simmer for 40-50 minutes or until tender.

3 Check the during cooking. If the stew need more liquid add a little stock. If you find there is too much, remove the lid and cook for a little longer to reduce the liquid.

4 Combine the tomatoes, sliced red onion & the rest of the olive oil together with a little salt and pepper. Serve in shallow bowls with the onion mix piled on top.

CHEFS NOTE
Back soy beans are a good low carb option

SHALLOT & SNOW PEA ONE-POT 'RISOTTO'

300 calories per serving

Ingredients

- 1 tbsp olive oil
- 12 shallots, chopped
- 1 leek, sliced
- 1 garlic clove, crushed
- 500g/1lb 2oz cauliflower 'rice'

- 200g/7oz snow peas
- 250g/3 cups vegetable stock
- 4 tbsp cream cheese
- Salt & pepper to taste

Method

1 Preheat the oven to 180c/350f/Gas4

2 Using a flameproof casserole dish gently sauté the shallots, leeks & garlic in the olive oil for about 5 minutes until softened.

3 Add the 'rice' and stir well for a minute or two until everything is coated with the olive oil.

4 Add the stock & snow peas and bring to the boil. Cover and place in the preheated oven for 25-30 minutes or until everthing is tender and the stock has been absorbed.

5 Check the 'risotto' during cooking. If it needs more liquid add a little stock. If you find there is too much, remove the lid and cook for a little longer to reduce the stock.

6 Remove from the oven, stir through the cream cheese, season & serve.

CHEFS NOTE
Try adding some Parmesan cheese or chopped basil to this simple keto 'risotto'.

COURGETTE & ENOKI STEW

340 calories per serving

Ingredients

- 2 onions, chopped
- 2 garlic cloves, crushed
- 300g/11oz courgettes/zucchini, sliced into batons
- 2 tbsp tomato puree/paste
- 400g/14oz tinned chopped tomatoes
- 120ml/½ cup vegetable stock
- 400g/14oz enoki mushrooms (chop half of them)
- 200g/7oz sugar snap
- Zest of one lemon
- Bunch freshly chopped basil
- 2 tsp olive oil
- Salt & pepper to taste

Method

1 Using a flameproof casserole dish, gently sauté the onions, garlic & courgettes in the oil for a few minutes until softened.

2 Add the puree, chopped tomatoes, stock, mushrooms, peas and lemon zest. Stir and leave to cook for a 20 minutes or until everything is tender and piping hot.

3 Check often during cooking. If it needs more liquid add a little stock. If you find there is too much, remove the lid and cook for a little longer to reduce the liquid.

4 Season and serve with chopped basil.

CHEFS NOTE
Enoki mushroms make a good keto base for this dish.

ASPARAGUS & SWEET POTATOES

340 calories per serving

Ingredients

- 1 red onion, chopped
- 2 garlic cloves, crushed
- 3 red peppers, deseeded & finely chopped
- 400g/14oz asparagus, chopped

- 3 large sweet potatoes, peeled & cubed
- 4 tbsp crème fraiche or sour cream
- 2 tsp olive oil
- Salt & pepper to taste

Method

1 Using a flameproof casserole dish, gently sauté the onions, garlic & peppers in the olive oil for a few minutes until softened.

2 Add the sweet potatoes and gently simmer for 15 minutes or until the sweet potatoes are just tender, quicky add the asaparagus and cook for 5 minutes more or until the asparagus is tender.

3 Check the casserole during cooking. If it needs seems to dry add a little stock.

4 Stir through the crème fraiche, season and serve.

CHEFS NOTE
Sweet potatoes are an acceptable 'occasional' keto ingredient.

ENOKI STILTON STEW

290 calories per serving

Ingredients

- 2 onions, sliced
- 2 celery stalks, chopped
- 2 garlic cloves, crushed
- 400g/14oz enoki mushrooms
- 1 tsp ground cumin

- 6 radishes, grated
- Large bunch spring onions/scallions finely chopped
- 2 tsp olive oil
- 75g/3oz stilton cheese

Method

1 Preheat the oven to 160c/325f/Gas3

2 Gently sauté the onions, celery, garlic & mushrooms in the olove oil for a few minutes until softened.

3 Add the cumin & cheese, combine well and place in the preheated oven to cook for 30 minutes or until the everything is tender and piping hot.

4 Season and serve in shallow bowls with grated radishes and chopped spring onions sprinkled over the top.

CHEFS NOTE

Chopped pumpkin seeds make a lovely additional garnish to this dish.

GOATS CHEESE & MUSHROOMS

310 calories per serving

Ingredients

- 50g/2oz porcini mushrooms
- 2 onions, sliced
- 2 garlic cloves, crushed
- 800g/1¾lb mixed mushrooms
- 2 tbsp tomato puree/paste

- 120ml/½ cup vegetable stock
- 1 tsp dried thyme
- 125g/4oz feta cheese, crumbled
- 2 tsp olive oil
- Salt & pepper to taste

Method

1 Soak the porcini mushrooms in a little warm water for 10 minutes until rehydrated. Drain and finely chop.

2 Using a flameproof casserole dish, gently sauté the onions, garlic, porcini mushrooms & mixed mushrooms in the oil for 10-15 minutes or until softened.

3 Stir through the tomato puree then add the stock and thyme. Bring to the boil, reduce the heat and simmer for 5-10 minutes or until the liquid has reduced by half.

4 Check during cooking. If it needs more liquid add a little stock. If you find there is too much, increase the heat to reduce the liquid.

5 Stir through the crumbled feta cheese, season and serve.

CHEFS NOTE
This is lovely served with steaming, buttery Savoy cabbage..

CALABRIAN STEW

290
calories per serving

Ingredients

- 1 tbsp olive oil
- 2 aubergine/egg plant, cubed
- 2 onions, sliced
- 4 garlic cloves, crushed
- 800g/1¾lb tinned chopped tomatoes
- 1 tsp brown sugar
- 150g/5oz pitted olives, sliced

- 1 tbsp capers, chopped
- 2 tbsp raisins, chopped
- 2 tbsp tomato puree/paste
- 2 tbsp balsamic vinegar
- 2 tbsp pine nuts
- Salt & pepper to taste

Method

1 Using a flameproof casserole dish, gently sauté the aubergine, onions & garlic in the olive oil for 10-15 minutes or until softened.

2 Add the chopped tomatoes, sugar, olives, capers, raisins, puree & vinegar. Bring to the boil, reduce the heat and simmer for 20-30 minutes or until the liquid has reduced by half.

3 Check often during cooking. If it needs more liquid add a little stock. If you find there is too much, increase the heat to reduce the liquid.

4 Meanwhile gently brown the pine nuts in a dry pan for a minute or two (don't let them burn.).

5 Season the stew and serve with the pine nuts sprinkled over the top.

CHEFS NOTE
This southern Italian stew is also good served with fresh basil or a dollop of green pesto.

SWEET POTATO & SOY BEAN DHAL

420 calories per serving

Ingredients

- 1 onion, sliced
- 1 green chilli, deseeded & finely sliced
- 1 tsp freshly grated ginger
- 2 celery stalks, chopped
- 2 garlic cloves, crushed
- 1 tbsp curry powder
- 1 tsp paprika
- 400g/14oz tinned chopped tomatoes

- 250g/9oz black soy beans
- 600g/1lb 5oz sweet potato, peeled & diced
- 1 vegetable stock cube, crumbled
- 250g/9oz green beans
- 2 tbsp lemon juice
- 2 tsp olive oil
- Salt & pepper to taste

Method

1 Gently sauté the onions, chilli, ginger, celery & garlic for a few minutes until softened (add a splash of water to the pan if it's a little dry).

2 Add the curry powder, paprika, chopped tomatoes, split peas, sweet potatoes & crumbled stock cube. Cover and gently simmer for 20 minutes.

3 Add the green beans and cook for 5 minutes longer or until the beans and sweet potatoes are tender.

4 Check the stew during cooking. If it needs more liquid add a little stock. If you find there is too much, remove the lid and cook for a little longer to reduce the liquid.

5 Season, stir through the lemon juice & serve.

CHEFS NOTE
Add a little freshly chopped coriander if you have any to hand.

OVEN BAKED PORCINI & TOMATO 'RISOTTO'

320 calories per serving

Ingredients

- 50g/2oz porcini mushrooms
- 1 tbsp olive oil
- 1 onion, chopped
- 1 leek, sliced
- 1 garlic clove, crushed

- 400g/14oz cherry tomatoes, halved
- 500g/1lb 2oz cauliflower 'rice'
- 120ml/ ½ cup vegetable stock
- Bunch fresh basil, chopped
- Salt & pepper to taste

Method

1 Preheat the oven to 180c/350f/Gas4

2 Soak the porcini mushrooms in a little warm water and leave to rehydrate for 10 minutes. Drain and finely chop.

3 Using a flameproof casserole dish gently sauté the onion, leek, garlic, tomatoes & porcini mushrooms in the olive oil for 5- 6 minutes until softened.

4 Add the cauliflower 'rice' and stir well for a minute or two until everything is coated with the olive oil.

5 Add the stock and bring to the boil. Cover and place in the preheated oven for 10 minutes or until the everything is tender and the stock has been absorbed.

6 Check the 'risotto' during cooking. If it needs more liquid add a little stock. If you find there is too much, remove the lid and cook for a little longer to reduce the stock.

7 Remove from the oven, season & serve with chopped basil.

CHEFS NOTE

You could also try some chopped sundried tomato in this veggie keto 'risotto'.

PAPRIKA POTATO GRATIN

260 calories per serving

Ingredients

- 1 tbsp olive oil
- 2 onions sliced
- 800g/1¾lb sweet potatoes, thinly sliced
- 1 tbsp paprika
- 370ml/1½ cups vegetable stock
- Salt & pepper to taste

Method

1 Preheat the oven to 180c/350f/Gas4

2 Brush a flameproof casserole with the olive oil. Layer the potatoes and onions in turn in the base of the dish. Pour over the stock and sprinkle the paprika on the top.

3 Cover and place in the oven for 1½-2 hours or until the potatoes are tender and the stock has been absorbed. Season & serve.

CHEFS NOTE
This versatile side dish is great served with lots of freshly grated black pepper.

BOMBAY ROAST POTATOES

175 calories per serving

Ingredients

- 1 tbsp olive oil
- 2 onions sliced
- 800g/1¾lb sweet potatoes, cubed
- 1 tbsp curry powder
- Salt & pepper to taste

TRY ADDING FRESH CHILLIES!

Method

1 Preheat the oven to 180c/350f/Gas4

2 Mix together the oil, onions, potatoes and curry powder.

3 Place in a flameproof casserole dish or roasting tin and cook in the preheated oven for 1-1 ½ hours or until the sweet potatoes are tender on the inside and crispy on the outside. Season & serve.

CHEFS NOTE
Serve this side dish with some freshly chopped coriander.

HARISSA 'COUSCOUS'

265 calories per serving

Ingredients

- 1 red onion, chopped
- 2 garlic cloves, crushed
- 1 red chilli, deseeded & finely sliced
- 1 red pepper, deseeded & finely chopped
- 2 tbsp harissa paste
- 800g/1¾lb tinned chopped tomatoes
- 3 tbsp lemon juice
- 500g/1lb 2oz cauliflower rice
- Bunch fresh coriander/cilantro, chopped
- 2 tsp olive oil
- Salt & pepper to taste

Method

1 Using a flameproof casserole dish, gently sauté the onions, garlic, chilli & peppers in the oil for a few minutes until softened.

2 Add the harissa paste & chopped tomatoes, cover and leave to gently simmer for 10-15 minutes.

3 Add the cauliflower 'rice' and cook for 5 minutes. leave for 5-10 minutes.

4 Fluff the 'couscous' with a fork, sprinkle with chopped coriander and lemon juice. Season & serve.

CHEFS NOTE

Harissa is an aromatic North African paste now widely available in most large food stores.

MUSHROOM & SWEET POTATO CURRY

340 calories per serving

Ingredients

- 1 onion, chopped
- 500g/1lb 2oz sweet potatoes, cubed
- 300g/11oz mushrooms, halved
- 1 red chilli, deseeded & sliced
- 2 tbsp Thai green curry paste
- 120ml/½ cup coconut milk
- 120ml/½ cup vegetable stock
- 125g/4oz spinach
- 2 tsp olive oil
- Salt & pepper to taste

Method

1 Using a flameproof casserole dish gently sauté the onions, potatoes, mushrooms & chillies in the oil for a few minutes until softened.

2 Add the curry paste, coconut milk & stock. Cover and leave to gently simmer for 10-15 minutes or until the potatoes are tender.

3 Stir through the spinach and serve immediately.

CHEFS NOTE
Sweet potatoes are ok on a keto diet as an 'occasional' ingredient.

MUSHROOM & SWEET POTATO CURRY

SERVES 4

Ingredients

Method

CHEF'S NOTE

KETO
ONE-POT
SEAFOOD
DISHES

SCOTS FISH STEW

470
calories per
serving

Ingredients

- 2 onions, chopped
- 800g/1¾lb sweet potatoes, peeled & diced
- 2 tsp butter spread
- 500ml/2 cups semi skimmed/half fat milk
- 500g/1lb 2oz boneless, smoked haddock, cubed
- Large pinch salt
- 2 tsp olive oil
- 2 tbsp freshly chopped flat leaf parsley
- 125g/4oz chopped spinach
- Salt & pepper to taste

Method

1 Using a flameproof casserole dish gently sauté the onions in the olive oil for a few minutes until softened.

2 Add the sweet potatoes & butter and sauté for a couple of minutes before adding the milk, fish & salt. Cover and leave to gently poach for 15-20 minutes or until the fish is cooked through and the potatoes are tender.

3 Check the stew during cooking; if it needs more liquid add some milk.

4 Stir through the spinach to wilt for a minute or two. Check the seasoning and serve with chopped parsley sprinkled over the top.

CHEFS NOTE
Crush some of the sweet potatoes with the back of a fork to thicken the sauce.

ALMOND & FISH ONE-POT

340
calories per
serving

Ingredients

- 2 onions, chopped
- 2 garlic cloves, crushed
- 2 red or yellow peppers, deseeded & sliced
- 400g/14oz tinned chopped tomatoes
- 2 tsp paprika
- 250ml/1 cup fish stock
- 2 tbsp ground almonds

- 750g/1lb 9oz boneless, white fish fillets, cubed
- Large pinch salt
- 2 tsp olive oil
- 2 tbsp freshly chopped flat leaf parsley
- Lemon wedges to serve
- Salt & pepper to taste

Method

1 Using a flameproof casserole dish gently sauté the onions, garlic & peppers in the olive oil for a few minutes until softened .

2 Add the chopped tomatoes, paprika, stock & almonds and combine well. Cover and cook for 10 minutes.

3 Add the fish and cook for a further 10 minutes or until the fish is cooked through.

4 Check the stew during cooking. If it needs more liquid add a little stock. If you find there is too much, remove the lid and cook for a little longer to reduce the liquid. Check the seasoning and serve with chopped parsley sprinkled over the top and lemon wedges on the side.

CHEFS NOTE
You could use any kind of seafood you prefer in this simple stew to create a more adventurous combination.

SHRIMP & CAULIFLOWER 'STEAK' STEW

430 calories per serving

Ingredients

- 2 onions, chopped
- 4 slices lean, back bacon chopped
- 2 garlic cloves, crushed
- 1 red pepper, deseeded & sliced
- 1 red chilli, deseeded & sliced
- 1 tsp turmeric
- 400g/14oz tinned chopped tomatoes
- 2 cauliflower cut into thick 'steaks'

- 250ml/1 cup fish stock
- 750g/1lb 11oz peeled king prawns
- Large pinch salt
- 2 tsp olive oil
- Salt & pepper to taste

Method

1 Using a flameproof casserole dish gently sauté the onions, bacon, garlic, peppers & chilli in the olive oil for a few minutes until softened.

2 Add the turmeric, chopped tomatoes, cauliflower & stock and combine well. Cover and cook for 10-15 minutes. Add the prawns and cook for a further 10 minutes or until cooked through.

3 Check the stew during cooking. If it needs more liquid add a little stock. If you find there is too much, remove the lid and cook for a little longer to reduce the liquid. Check the seasoning and serve.

CHEFS NOTE
A garnish of freshly chopped thyme makes a good addition to this dish.

SALTED COD & CHERRY TOMATO STEW

497 calories per serving

Ingredients

- 1 onion, chopped, finely sliced
- 400g/14oz ripe cherry tomatoes, halved
- 2 celery stalks, chopped
- 3 garlic cloves, crushed
- 1 red pepper, deseeded & sliced
- 2 tsp paprika
- 250ml/1 cup fish stock

- 400g/14oz tinned white kidney beans
- 750g/1lb 11oz pre soaked salt cod fillet, cubed
- Large pinch salt
- 2 tsp olive oil
- Salt & pepper to taste

Method

1 Using a flameproof casserole dish gently sauté the onions, cherry tomatoes, celery, garlic, peppers & paprika in the olive oil for a few minutes until softened.

2 Add the stock and leave on a medium simmer for 20 minutes, don't cover the stew as you want the liquid to reduce down.

3 Add the beans and salt cod, cover and leave to gently cook for a further 10-15 minutes or until the fish is cooked through and the beans are piping hot. Check the seasoning and serve.

CHEFS NOTE
Make sure the salt cod is properly soaked overnight in cold water.

SEAFOOD 'RICE' ONE-POT

455 calories per serving

Ingredients

- 1 onion, chopped
- 3 garlic cloves, crushed
- 125g/4oz chorizo, finely chopped
- 1 red pepper, deseeded & sliced
- ½ red chilli, deseeded & finely chopped
- 200g/7oz cherry tomatoes, halved
- 250ml/1 cup chicken or fish stock
- 400g/14oz cauliflower rice
- Pinch of saffron strands
- 2 tbsp lemon juice
- 150g/5oz green beans, chopped
- 200g/7oz squid cleaned and sliced
- 200g/7oz shelled king prawns, chopped
- 2 tsp olive oil
- Salt & pepper to taste

Method

1 Using a heavy bottomed frying pan gently sauté the onions, garlic, chorizo, peppers, chilli & cherry tomatoes in the olive oil for a few minutes until softened.

2 Add the stock, saffronm lemon juice and bring to the boil.

3 Add the green beans, cauliflower rice, squid & prawns, cover and leave to simmer for 8-10 minutes or until the prawns & squid are cooked through.

4 Check the paella during cooking. If it needs more liquid add additional stock. Season and serve.

CHEFS NOTE
Adjust the chilli to suit your own taste.

INDIAN COD & SPINACH STEW

390 calories per serving

Ingredients

- 2 onions, chopped
- 2 garlic cloves, crushed
- 1 tsp freshly grated ginger
- 400g/14oz ripe cherry tomatoes, halved
- 400g/14oz black soy beans
- 1 tbsp medium curry powder
- 250ml/1 cup fish or chicken stock
- 200g/7oz spinach leaves

- 600g/1lb 5oz boneless, white fish fillets, cubed
- Large pinch salt
- 2 tsp olive oil
- 2 tbsp freshly chopped flat leaf parsley
- Lemon wedges to serve
- Salt & pepper to taste

Method

1 Using a flameproof casserole dish gently sauté the onions, garlic & ginger in the olive oil for a few minutes until softened.

2 Add the cherry tomatoes, soy beans, curry powder & stock and combine well. Cook for 10 minutes on a hard simmer, add the fish and cook for a further 10 minutes or until the fish is cooked through.

3 Stir through the spinach for a minute or two until it is properly wilted. Check the seasoning and serve with lemon wedges on the side.

CHEFS NOTE

Black soy beans are a good low carb stew ingredient.

SALMON & FENNEL STEW

395 calories per serving

Ingredients

- 2 onions, chopped
- 2 garlic cloves, crushed
- 200g/7oz broccoli, broken into small florets
- 1 fennel bulb, finely chopped
- 3 tbsp tomato puree
- 400g/14oz sweet potatoes, peeled & cubed
- 250ml/1 cup fish or chicken stock
- 200g/7oz green beans
- 600g/1lb 5oz boneless, salmon fillets, cubed
- Large pinch salt
- 2 tsp olive oil
- Lemon wedges to serve
- Salt & pepper to taste

Method

1 Using a flameproof casserole dish gently sauté the onions, garlic, broccoli & chopped fennel in the olove oil for a few minutes until softened.

2 Add the puree, sweet potatoes & stock and combine well. Cook for 10 minutes on a hard simmer.

3 Add the green beans & salmon, cover and leave to gently simmer for further 10 minutes or until the fish is cooked through and the sweet potatoes are tender.

4 Check the seasoning and serve with lemon wedges on the side.

CHEFS NOTE

Serve this stew with lots of freshly ground black pepper.

MUSSEL & OKRA STEW

420 calories per serving

Ingredients

- 2 onions, chopped
- 2 garlic cloves, crushed
- 2 carrots, finely diced
- 400g/14oz okra, peeled & cubed
- 100g/3½oz green beans, chopped
- 1lt/4 cups fish stock

- 1 tbsp curry powder
- 1kg/2¼lb cleaned, prepared mussels
- 120ml/½ cup single cream
- 2 tsp olive oil
- Lemon wedges to serve
- Salt & pepper to taste

Method

1 Using a flameproof casserole dish gently sauté the onions, garlic, carrots, okra & green beans in the olive oil for approx. 10 minutes or until the okra is tender.

2 While you are doing this bring the stock and curry powder to the boil in another pan & cook the mussels for 4-5 minutes or until their shells open. (Get rid of any mussels that don't open).

3 Remove a ladle of stock and add to the casserole dish along with cooked mussels. Combine everything well, stir through the cream, warm for a minute or two and serve.

CHEFS NOTE
Serve with slices of almond flour bread to mop up the creamy juices.

MARRAKESH STEW

483
calories per
serving

Ingredients

- 2 onions, chopped
- 2 garlic cloves, crushed
- 200g/7oz mushrooms, sliced
- 400g/14oz tinned chopped tomatoes
- 300g/11oz tinned white kidney beans
- 1 tsp each turmeric, cumin & ground coriander/cilantro

- Pinch cinnamon & nutmeg
- 1 tbsp honey
- 500g/1lb 2oz shelled king prawns
- 2 tsp olive oil
- Lemon wedges to serve
- Salt & pepper to taste

Method

1 Using a flameproof casserole dish gently sauté the onions, garlic & mushrooms in the olove oil for a few minutes until softened.

2 Add the chopped tomatoes, beans, ground spices & honey to the casserole. Combine well, cover and cook for 30 minutes.

3 Add the prawns and gently simmer for a further 10 minutes or until the prawns are cooked through.

4 Check the stew during cooking. If it needs more liquid add a little stock. If you find there is too much, remove the lid and cook for a little longer to reduce the liquid. Check the seasoning and serve.

CHEFS NOTE
Unlike many other beans, white kidney beans are a good low carb stew ingredient.

SLOW COOKED SQUID

390 calories per serving

Ingredients

- 2 onions, chopped
- 2 garlic cloves, crushed
- 800g/1¾lb tinned chopped tomatoes
- 3 tbsp tomato puree
- ½ red chilli deseeded & finely chopped
- Pinch salt & brown sugar
- 1 tsp paprika
- 1 tsp anchovy paste
- 500g/1lb 2oz prepared squid, sliced into 1cm/½ inch pieces
- 500g/1lb 2oz enoki mushrooms
- Bunch flat leaf parsley, chopped
- 2 tsp olive oil
- Salt & pepper to taste

Method

1 Using a flameproof casserole dish gently sauté the onions & garlic in the olive oil for a few minutes until softened.

2 Add the chopped tomatoes, puree, chilli, salt, sugar, paprika & anchovy paste. Combine well, cover and cook for 10 minutes on a medium heat.

3 After this time place the sauce in a food processor or blender and whizz until smooth. Return the blended sauce back to the casserole and add the squid. Cover and leave to gently simmer for about 50 minutes.

4 Add the mushrooms, cover and cook for a further 10-15 minute or until everything is piping hot and the squid is tender.

5 Check the stew during cooking. If it needs more liquid add a little stock. If you find there is too much, remove the lid and cook for a little longer to reduce the liquid. Check the seasoning and serve with chopped flat leaf parsley sprinkled on top.

CHEFS NOTE

The squid should be really tender after an hour of slow cooking. Leave it to cook for longer if needed.

MIXED SEAFOOD STEW

295 calories per serving

Ingredients

- 2 onions, chopped
- 2 garlic cloves, crushed
- 120ml/½ cup white wine
- 1 tsp fennel seeds
- 400g/14oz tinned chopped tomatoes
- 120ml/½ cup tomato pasatta/sauce

- ½ red chilli deseeded & finely chopped
- Pinch salt & brown sugar
- 700g/1lb 9oz mixed seafood, cubed
- Bunch fresh chopped chives
- 2 tsp olove oil
- Salt & pepper to taste

Method

1 Using a flameproof casserole dish gently sauté the onions & garlic in the olove oil for a few minutes until softened.

2 Add the wine & fennel seeds and bring to the boil. Simmer on high for 3-5 minutes or until most of the wine has reduced.

3 Add the chopped tomatoes, passata, chilli, salt, sugar & seafood. Combine well, cover and cook for 15-20 minutes on a gentle heat.

4 Check the seasoning and serve with chopped chives sprinkled on top.

CHEFS NOTE
White wine is acceptable as an 'occasional' keto cooking ingredient

MONKFISH & MUSHROOM STEW

385 calories per serving

Ingredients

- 1 onion, chopped
- 2 garlic cloves, crushed
- 1 pumpkin, finely chopped
- ½ tsp fennel seeds
- 400g/14oz tinned chopped tomatoes
- 250ml/1 cup fish stock
- ½ red chilli deseeded & finely chopped

- 50g/2oz porcini mushrooms
- 200g/7oz mushrooms, sliced
- Pinch salt & brown sugar
- 700g/1lb 9oz monkfish fillets, cubed
- 2 tsp olive oil
- Salt & pepper to taste

Method

1 Soak the porcini mushrooms in a little warm water for a few minutes until rehydrated, drain and finely chop.

2 Using a flameproof casserole dish gently sauté the onions, garlic & pumpkin in the olive oil for a few minutes until softened.

3 Add the stock & fennel seeds and bring to the boil. Simmer on high for 3-5 minutes until most of the wine has reduced.

4 Add the chopped tomatoes, chilli, porcini mushrooms, sliced mushrooms, salt, sugar & monkfish.

5 Combine well, cover and cook for 30-40 minutes on a very gentle heat. Check the acidity of the tomato base and balance with a little more salt or sugar if needed.

CHEFS NOTE
You could leave the monkfish in whole fillets if you like and serve on a bed of fresh spinach.

ZESTY PRAWN & LEEK ONE-POT

330 calories per serving

Ingredients

- 1 onion, chopped, finely sliced
- 2 leeks, finely sliced
- 400g/14oz ripe cherry tomatoes, halved
- 120ml/½ cup fish stock
- 400g/14oz tinned black soy beans, drained
- 600g/1lb 5oz shelled king prawns
- Zest of one lemon
- 2 tsp olive oil
- Salt & pepper to taste

Method

1 Using a flameproof casserole dish gently sauté the onions & leeks in the olive oil for a few minutes until softened.

2 Add the tomatoes & fish stock, cover and cook for 40 minutes until the tomatoes break down.

3 Add the beans & prawns, cover and leave to gently cook for a further 10 minutes or until the prawns are cooked through and the beans are piping hot.

4 Stir through the lemon zest, check the seasoning and serve.

CHEFS NOTE
Use meaty white fish fillets instead of prawns if you prefer.

SUPER QUICK TUNA 'STEW' ON 'TOAST'

430 calories per serving

Ingredients

- 1 onion, finely sliced
- 100g/3½oz pitted black olives, halved
- ½ tsp brown sugar
- 600g/1lb 5oz fresh tuna steak, cut into strips
- 5 large vine ripened tomatoes, roughly chopped
- 60ml/¼ cup fish stock
- 60ml/¼ cup soy sauce
- 4 slices thick almond flour bread, lightly toasted
- 2 tsp olive oil
- Salt & pepper to taste

Method

1 Using a frying pan gently sauté the onion, olives & sugar the olive oil for a few minutes until softened.

2 Add the tuna, tomatoes, stock & soy sauce, combine well and cook for 4-6 minutes or until the tuna is cooked through.

3 Check the seasoning and serve on top of the toasted almond bread slices.

CHEFS NOTE
A tablespoon of chopped capers makes a great addition to this super-quick dish.

PRAWN & SQUASH ASIAN ONE-POT

350 calories per serving

Ingredients

- 2 onions, chopped
- 2 garlic cloves, crushed
- 1 butternut squash, peeled, deseeded & cubed
- 1 tbsp fish sauce
- 1 tbsp Thai red curry paste
- 1 tbsp lime pickle

- 120ml/½ cup coconut milk
- 200g/7oz green beans
- 600g/1lb 5oz shelled, king prawns
- 2 tsp olive oil
- Lemon wedges to serve
- Salt & pepper to taste

Method

1 Using a flameproof casserole dish gently sauté the onions, garlic & chopped squash in the olive oil for a few minutes until softened.

2 Add the fish sauce, curry paste, lime pickle & coconut milk. Cover and gently simmer for 20 minutes. Add the green beans & prawns, cover and leave to gently simmer for a further 10 minutes or until the prawns are cooked through and the squash is tender.

3 Check the seasoning and serve.

CHEFS NOTE
This dish is lovely served with beansprouts and chopped coriander.

SPANISH SEAFOOD LOW CARB BEANS

350 calories per serving

Ingredients

- 1 tbsp olive oil
- 3 red peppers, deseeded & sliced
- 1 onion, chopped
- 2 garlic cloves, crushed
- 400g/14oz white kidney beans
- 250g/1 cup vegetable stock
- 2 tsp paprika
- 1 tsp turmeric
- 750g/1lb 11oz shelled prawns, chopped
- Salt & pepper to taste

Method

1 Preheat the oven to 180c/350f/Gas4

2 Using a flameproof casserole dish gently sauté the peppers, onion & garlic in the olive oil for about 5 minutes until softened.

3 Add the beans and stir well.

4 Add the stock, paprika & turmeric and bring to the boil. . Add the prawns, place in the oven and cook for 10-20 minutes or until the the stock has been absorbed and the prawns are cooked through.

5 Check during cooking. If it needs more liquid add a little stock. If you find there is too much, remove the lid and cook for a little longer to reduce the stock.

6 Remove from the oven, season & serve.

CHEFS NOTE
You could also add some chopped chorizo to this Spanish dish.

LOW CARB KEDGEREE

380 calories per serving

Ingredients

- 1 onion, chopped
- 2 garlic cloves, crushed
- 1 tsp turmeric
- 400g/14oz cauliflower 'rice'
- 150g/5oz sugar snap peas
- 400g/14oz smoked haddock, cut into chunks
- 8 hardboiled eggs, chopped
- 250ml/1 cup fish or chicken stock
- Bunch spring onions/scallions, chopped
- Bunch flat leaf parsley, chopped
- 2 tsp olive oil
- Salt & pepper to taste

Method

1 Preheat the oven to 180c/350f/Gas4

2 Using a flameproof casserole dish gently sauté the onions & garlic in the olive oil for a few minutes until the onions are softened.

3 Add the turmeric, 'rice', peas & stock and cook for a few minutes. Cover and place in the preheated oven for 10 minutes.

4 Add the haddock and combine well. Cover and cook for a further 10-15 minutes or until the haddock is cooked through and the stock has been absorbed.

5 Check the kedgeree during cooking. If it needs more liquid add a little stock. If you find there is too much, remove the lid and cook for a little longer to reduce the liquid.

6 Meanwhile mix together the chopped eggs, spring onion & parsley. When the kedgeree is cooked stir the egg and onion mixture through the rice. Season and serve.

CHEFS NOTE

Try adding a little paprika to the egg & onion mixture.

BONUS
KETO
SMOOTHIES
+DRINKS

RASPBERRY AND CREAM CHEESE SMOOTHIE

149 calories per serving

Ingredients

- 60g/2½oz raspberries
- 25g/1oz cream cheese
- 250ml/1 cup almond milk
- 1 tbsp sugar-free vanilla syrup

Method

1 Tip the raspberries into your blender.

2 Add the cream cheese then pour in the almond milk and the syrup.

3 Blend until smooth. Add water if you wish.

4 Pour into a glass and enjoy!

CHEFS NOTE

A delicious and filling smoothie with less than 4 carbs. Use either fresh or frozen raspberries, and if you can't get vanilla syrup from your local shop, it's available from online retailers.

RHUBARB AND STRAWBERRY SMOOTHIE

320 calories per serving

Ingredients

- 50g/2oz rhubarb, roughly chopped
- 40g/1½oz strawberries
- 5 almonds
- 1 tsp freshly grated ginger
- 120ml/½ cup unsweetened almond milk

- 2 tbsp double cream
- ½ tsp vanilla extract
- 5 drops liquid sweetener

Method

1 Tip the strawberries, rhubarb and almonds into your blender.

2 Add the ginger, then pour in the almond milk, cream, vanilla extract and sweetener.

3 Blend until smooth. Add water if you wish.

4 Pour into a glass and serve.

CHEFS NOTE
Use almond butter instead of almonds if you prefer.

AVOCADO AND ALMOND SMOOTHIE

440 calories per serving

Ingredients

- 1 tbsp chia seeds
- 3 tbsp water
- ½ avocado, stoned, frozen
- 1 tbsp almond butter

- 2 tsp cocoa powder
- 250ml/1 cup unsweetened almond milk
- 1 tbsp coconut oil, melted
- A few ice cubes

Method

1 Soak the chia seeds in the water for 10 minutes, then tip them into your blender.

2 Add the avocado, almond butter and cocoa.

3 Pour in the almond milk and coconut oil.

4 Add a few ice cubes, if you wish.

5 Blend until smooth, then pour into a glass and serve.

CHEFS NOTE
High fat, high protein, low carb – and delicious! Feel free to substitute the nut milk and butter – e.g. try with coconut instead of almond.

GREEN DETOX SMOOTHIE

480 calories per serving

Ingredients

- 40g/2½oz lettuce
- 25g/1oz blackberries
- 75g/3oz cucumber, chopped
- 1 kiwi fruit, peeled and chopped
- 1 tbsp fresh parsley

- ½ avocado, stoned. peeled & roughly chopped
- 2 tsp freshly grated ginger,
- 1 tbsp sweetener
- 500ml/2 cups coconut milk

Method

1 Drop the lettuce, blackberries, cucumber, kiwi and avocado into your blender.

2 Add the parsley, ginger and sweetener and pour in the water.

3 Blend until smooth.

4 Pour into 2 or 3 glasses and serve.

CHEFS NOTE

A great detox, low carb smoothie to start your day.

RASPBERRY AND NUT SMOOTHIE

304 calories per serving

Ingredients

- 125g/4oz raspberries
- 50g/2oz almond flour
- 2 tbsp peanut butter
- 225g/8oz Greek yogurt
- 125ml/½ cup unsweetened almond milk
- 1 tsp sweetener
- 4 ice cubes

Method

1 Tip the raspberries and flour into your blender.

2 Add the peanut butter and yogurt and then pour in the almond milk. Add the sweetener.

3 Blend until smooth.

4 Add the ice and blend again until completely smooth.

5 Add water if you wish. Pour into 2 glasses and serve immediately.

CHEFS NOTE
Omit the ice if your blender can't handle it – the smoothie will still taste great.

STRAWBERRY MINT SMOOTHIE

420 calories per serving

Ingredients

- 5 frozen strawberries
- Fresh mint leaves
- 250ml/1 cup coconut milk
- 1 tbsp sugar-free vanilla syrup

Method

1 Tip the strawberries into your blender with the mint.

2 Pour in the coconut milk and syrup.

3 Blend until smooth. Add water if you wish

4 Pour into a glass and enjoy!

CHEFS NOTE

For a lower calorie count try with almond milk or cow's milk if you prefer.

MATCHA MILK

177 calories per serving

Ingredients

- 250ml/1 cup unsweetened cashew milk
- 1 tbsp coconut oil, melted
- 1 tsp matcha powder
- ¼ tsp vanilla seeds (or vanilla extract)
- 2 ice cubes
- Sprinkling cocoa powder

Method

1 Pour the cashew milk into your blender with the coconut oil.

2 Add the matcha powder and vanilla, then drop in a couple of ice cubes.

3 Blend until the drink is the consistency you want.

4 Pour it into a glass and sprinkle a little cocoa powder on top.

5 Drink!

CHEFS NOTE

Among other health benefits, matcha is rich in dietary fibre and antioxidants. It also helps boost the metabolism and burn calories.

BUTTERY HOT CHOCOLATE

189
calories per serving

Ingredients

- 15g/½oz unsalted butter
- 2 tbsp cocoa powder
- ½ tsp vanilla extract

- 250ml/1 cup boiling water
- 2 tbsp double cream, whipped

Method

1 Add the butter, cocoa and vanilla to a large mug.

2 Pour the boiling water in and mix vigorously. Use a hand blender if you wish.

3 When the top is foamy, add the cream. Enjoy!

CHEFS NOTE

You can use coconut cream instead, or leave the cream out altogether if you wish – it's still delicious keto goodness.

CONVERSION CHART: DRY INGREDIENTS

Metric	Imperial
7g	¼ oz
15g	½ oz
20g	¾ oz
25g	1 oz
40g	1½oz
50g	2oz
60g	2½oz
75g	3oz
100g	3½oz
125g	4oz
140g	4½oz
150g	5oz
165g	5½oz
175g	6oz
200g	7oz
225g	8oz
250g	9oz
275g	10oz
300g	11oz
350g	12oz
375g	13oz
400g	14oz

Metric	Imperial
425g	15oz
450g	1lb
500g	1lb 2oz
550g	1¼lb
600g	1lb 5oz
650g	1lb 7oz
675g	1½lb
700g	1lb 9oz
750g	1lb 11oz
800g	1¾lb
900g	2lb
1kg	2¼lb
1.1kg	2½lb
1.25kg	2¾lb
1.35kg	3lb
1.5kg	3lb 6oz
1.8kg	4lb
2kg	4½lb
2.25kg	5lb
2.5kg	5½lb
2.75kg	6lb

CONVERSION CHART: LIQUID MEASURES

Metric	Imperial	US
25ml	1fl oz	
60ml	2fl oz	¼ cup
75ml	2½ fl oz	
100ml	3½fl oz	
120ml	4fl oz	½ cup
150ml	5fl oz	
175ml	6fl oz	
200ml	7fl oz	
250ml	8½ fl oz	1 cup
300ml	10½ fl oz	
360ml	12½ fl oz	
400ml	14fl oz	
450ml	15½ fl oz	
600ml	1 pint	
750ml	1¼ pint	3 cups
1 litre	1½ pints	4 cups